Lost for Words

Creative messages for all occasions

Kathy Schmidt and Louise Jourdan

NEW HOLLAND

First published in Australia in 2005 by
New Holland Publishers (Australia) Pty Ltd
Sydney • Auckland • London • Cape Town

1/66 Gibbes St, Chatswood, NSW 2067 Australia
218 Lake Road Northcote Auckland New Zealand
86 Edgware Road London W2 2EA United Kingdom
80 McKenzie Street Cape Town 8001 South Africa

National Library of Australia Cataloguing-in-Publication Data:
Schmidt, Kathy, 1967- .
  Lost for words : creative and inspirational messages for
  all occasions.

  ISBN 9781741103144

  1. Inspiration - Quotations, maxims, etc. 2. Anecdotes. 3.
  Quotations, English. I. Jourdan, Louise, 1975- . II.
  Title.

  808.882

Publisher: Fiona Schultz
Managing Editor: Lliane Clarke
Editor: Liz Hardy
Designer: Nanette Backhouse
Production Manager: Olga Dementiev
Printer: McPherson's Printing Group, Victoria

Contents

PREFACE

'All of us are walking around with some kind of birthday card we would like to give—some personal expression of joy, creativity or aliveness that we are hiding under our shirt.'
—Unknown

Have you ever bought a card for a friend or family member and been at a total loss for words? It is a familiar situation for all of us. We sit with our pen poised over the card for 20 minutes waiting for that lightning bolt of inspiration to flow through the pen and onto the card with something intelligent, amusing, caring or sympathetic. We want the receiver to be so moved by our words that they will want to keep it for eternity rather than discard it discreetly after a few days.

But in a last minute dash, and out of desperation, our master-piece is more like:

To ....

Best wishes

From ....

It's a pretty poor effort, but we are not alone. Don't be afraid any longer of buying the perfect card that is blank inside. Let this book be your lifesaver and give you inspiration.

Birthday

*'Let us celebrate the occasion
with wine and sweet words.'*

— Plautus
(254—184 BC, Roman comic dramatist)

Today, on your birthday, I look back on all the times
I have been touched by your kindness.

✍

On your birthday, I want to thank you for making
such a beautiful difference in my life.

✍

I am so blessed that I have been part of your life for another year.

✍

Though we celebrate your birthday today, we have reason to celebrate
every day for having someone as wonderful as you in our lives.

✍

I hope you have a fantastic birthday. Thank you for being
such a wonderful friend and for all your support. I look
forward to many more years of friendship.

✍

With love on your special day.

✍

I hope you have a great birthday filled with many surprises.

✍

I hope it will be a special and memorable day.

✍

Happy birthday to my disco diva.

✍

May your birthday be everything beautiful,
everything special, everything happy.

✍

Have a happy day, celebrating with family and friends
and reminiscing about birthdays gone by.

May happiness be in your heart on your birthday and always.

✍

It's your [age] birthday. I wish you many more
birthdays to come.

✍

We hope you really enjoyed your [age] birthday and
we are glad we could celebrate it with you.

✍

Happy [age] birthday. Things keep getting better and better.

✍

You have achieved so much in your first [age] years and
I am looking forward to what is yet to come.

✍

On your birthday, I want you to know how blessed
I am to have you in my life.

✍

Don't think of yourself as going to seed ... think of yourself
as being ready to blossom! Happy birthday.

✍

On your birthday, some words of wisdom: smile
while you still have teeth! Happy birthday.

✍

To my dear friend, who was born in the days when things
were made to last, you don't look a day over [age] .

✍

You know you're getting older when your knees
buckle and your belt won't. Happy birthday.

Don't do anything embarrassing on your birthday this year.
You don't have as much time to live it down as you used to.

✍

I realise that getting old can seem intimidating at first.
But what's it like now? Happy birthday.

✍

Honey, I knew you'd appreciate a relaxing, home-cooked
meal for your birthday. So I called your mother and
she said Wednesday was fine.

✍

Don't worry, sister, you're not getting older ... just more like mum.

✍

As we grow older, we often find that it is better to light one small candle than to be seen in fluorescent lighting. Happy birthday.

✍

You know you're getting older when your children
begin to look middle-aged.

✍

You're not getting a year older. You're getting another
year to shop! Happy birthday.

BIRTHDAY QUOTES

'Our birthdays are feathers in the broad wing of time.'
—Johann Friedrich Richter (1763–1825), German author

'Birthdays? yes, in a general way;
For the most if not for the best of men:
You were born (I suppose) on a certain day:
So was I: or perhaps in the night: what then?'
—James Kenneth Stephen (1859–92), British poet

'From our birthday, until we die,
Is but the winking of an eye.'
—William Butler Yeats (1865–1939), Irish poet

'There are three hundred and sixty-four days when
you might get un-birthday presents ... and only one
for birthday presents, you know.'
—Lewis Carroll (1832–98), British writer and mathematician

'Old age: A great sense of calm and freedom. When the
passions have relaxed their hold, you may have escaped,
not from one master but from many.'
—Plato (427–347 BC), Greek philosopher

'... the birthday of my life
Is come, my love is come to me.'
—Christina Georgina Rossetti (1830–94), British poet

'One of the signs of passing youth is the birth of a sense
of fellowship with other human beings as we take our
place among them.'
—Virginia Woolf (1882–1941), British novelist

'The greatest comfort of my old age, and that which gives me the highest satisfaction, is the pleasing remembrance of the many benefits and friendly offices I have done to others.'
— Marcus Cato (95-46BC), Roman statesman, soldier and Stoic philosopher

'May you live all the days of your life.'
— Jonathan Swift (1667—1745), British satirical writer, born in Ireland

'Grow old along with me! The best is yet to be, the last of life, for which the first was made.'
— Robert Browning (1812—89), British poet

FUNNY BIRTHDAY QUOTES

'Inside every older person is a younger person wondering what the hell happened.'
— Cora Harvey Armstrong, US gospel singer

'To me, old age is always fifteen years older than I am.'
— Bernard Mannes Baruch (1870—1965), US politician and financier

'Of late I appear
To have reached that stage
When people look old
Who are only my age.'
— Richard Armour (1906—89), US poet and humorist

'A diplomat is a man who always remembers a woman's birthday but never remembers her age.'
— Robert Frost (1874—1963), US poet

'You are only young once, but you can be immature for a lifetime.'
— John P. Grier, unknown

'If I'd known I was going to live this long,
I'd have taken better care of myself.'
  —Eubie Blake (1883—1983), US musician,
    on his 100th birthday

'Men are like wine. Some turn to vinegar,
but the best improve with age.'
  —C.E.M. Joad (1891—1953), British broadcaster
    and philosopher

'Let us respect grey hairs, especially our own.'
  —J.P. Sears, unknown

'Age is a high price to pay for maturity.'
  —Tom Stoppard (born 1937), British playwright,
    born in Czechoslovakia

'If we could be twice young and twice old
we could correct all our mistakes.'
  —Euripides (480—406? BC), Athenian tragician

'Growing old is like being increasingly
penalised for a crime you have not committed.'
  —Anthony Dymoke Powell (1905—2000), British author

CHILD'S BIRTHDAY

Have a great birthday and eat lots of cake.

✍

May your birthday be a happy day with lots of fun and may
it bring all the things that birthday girls/boys love.

✍

Have a wonderful day you gorgeous girl/beautiful boy.

To my lovely (granddaughter/son, little friend, niece/nephew).
I love you very much. Have a wonderful birthday.

✍

May all your birthday wishes come true.
Have a wonderful day and enjoy your present.

✍

Have a super, wonderful, fabulous, fantastic, totally
cool birthday. May you be spoiled rotten!

✍

Wishing you a special day when
everything goes your way.

✍

[Number] candles on a cake ... Have a great day.

✍

A special day with gifts and friends. You deserve
this and so much more.

✍

Hoping every day is full of new adventures. Have fun being [age].

✍

We hope you enjoy your [age] birthday and all your
pressies, cake, lollies and all the other stuff involved
with these things called 'birthdays'.

✍

Happy Birthday—you're [age]. We hope you have fun
with your family and all your friends.

✍

We hope you have lots of fun and get loads of pressies.

Lots of laughs and lots of fun on the happiest
day of the year, your birthday.

✍

A lifetime of joy and happiness to you.

30TH AND 35TH BIRTHDAY QUOTES

'*Everything I know I learned after I was thirty.*'
  —Georges Clemenceau (1841–1929), French politician

'*Time and Tide wait for no man, but time always
stands still for a woman of thirty.*'
  —Robert Frost (1874–1963), US poet

'*Thirty-five is when you finally get your head together
and your body starts falling apart.*'
  —Caryn Leschen, US graphic artist

'*Thirty-five is a very attractive age; London society
is full of women who have of their own free choice
remained thirty-five for years.*'
  —Oscar Wilde (1854–1900), Irish dramatist and novelist

40TH BIRTHDAY QUOTES

'*Life begins at forty.*'
  —W.B. Pitkin (1878–1953), US writer

50TH BIRTHDAY QUOTES

*'The years between fifty and seventy are the hardest.
You are always being asked to do things, and yet you
are not decrepit enough to turn them down.'*
—TS Eliot (1888–1965), British poet

60TH BIRTHDAY QUOTES

*'A man of sixty has spent twenty years in bed
and over three years in eating.'*
—Arnold Bennett (1867–1931), English novelist

MIDDLE AGE QUOTES

*'Middle age: When you begin to exchange your
emotions for symptoms.'*
—Georges Clemenceau (1841–1929), French politician

*'Middle age occurs when you are too young to take up
golf and too old to rush up to the net.'*
—Franklin Pierce Adams (1881–1960), US columnist

OLD AGE QUOTES

'Nobody loves life like him that's growing old'
  —Sophocles (495—406? BC), Greek tragedian

'The greatest problem about old age is the fear
that it may go on too long.'
  —A.J.P. Taylor (1906—90), British historian

'Old age is the most unexpected of all things
that happens to a man.'
  —Leon Trotsky (1879—1940), Russian revolutionary leader

'Don't look back. Something might be gaining on you.'
  —Satchel Paige (1906—82), US baseball pitcher

'Old age isn't so bad when you consider the alternative.'
  —Maurice Chevalier (1888—1972), French actor and singer

'Youth is a blunder; manhood a struggle; old age a regret.'
  —Benjamin Disraeli (1804—81), British politician and novelist

Valentines

'For, you see, each day I love you more,
today more than yesterday
and less than tomorrow.'

—Rosemonde Gerard (1871–1953),
US writer

I think I have found my friend for life.

✍

My heart skips a beat every time I think of you and the times we have shared. I'll never let you go.

✍

I really want you to know you're my special someone ... a cool breeze on a hot day.

✍

You're the only one for me. I long for a place in your heart. When I see your face I know the future is bright.

✍

My first thoughts of the day are always of you.

✍

For you there is nothing I would not do, as your love is etched upon my heart.

✍

To my beautiful wife/girlfriend who is always spending her love with kind and thoughtful gestures.

✍

You are like a beautiful diamond, admired and precious.

✍

You have touched my heart in a way no-one else has or ever could. You're the fire in my heart. I'll love you always.

✍

My eyes are drawn to your breath-taking beauty.

✍

To the woman who captured my love and admiration.

Thinking of you brings such warmth to my heart ...
no-one can compare to you or the love we share.

✍

Words cannot describe the overwhelming feelings of
love and passion I have for you.

✍

You transport me to paradise. You transform my
dreams and aspirations.
I did not know that such love could exist till I met you.

✍

I want to hold you close, care for you, protect you
and love you always.

✍

The love I have within my heart will last forever.

✍

In my heart I keep the sparkle of your eyes and your warm smile.

✍

To my warm, vibrant and intelligent girlfriend/boyfriend/
husband/wife. You grow more special to me every day.

✍

Even though we may be apart, you are always with me.
I would send you a kiss but the postman might steal it.

✍

I just wanted to say, I think you're special every day.

✍

Sweetpea, you have stolen my heart.

✍

You make me the man/woman I am. I give you my heart.

My deepest thoughts are always of you.

If you will just be mine, we will never part.

Let me give you my arms so I can hold you forever.

I would walk a thousand miles just to spend
all my days with you by my side.

When I think of love I think of you and your radiant smile.

It has been said it is impossible to love and be wise.
But for you I can't help but to love.

I once heard love ceases to be a pleasure when it ceases to be
a secret. Happy Valentine's Day, love your secret admirer.

May our hearts touch softly on this special day.

Beautiful girl ... I will love you forever.

I am so happy you came into my life with all your beautiful qualities.

With you in my life, I awake each day happy.

I will always be yours and you will always be mine.

VALENTINE QUOTES

'Life has taught us that love does not consist in gazing at each other but in looking outward together in the same direction.'
—Antoine de Saint-Exupéry (1900—44), French pilot and poet

'I arise from dreams of thee
In the first sweet sleep of night,
When the winds are breathing low,
And the stars are shining bright.'
—Percy Bysshe Shelley (1792—1822), British poet

Engagement

How happy you both must be. Congratulations.

✍

The very warmest wishes. May both of you
enjoy this day of happy celebrations.

✍

We see the magic in both of you. Congratulations
and looking forward to your special day.

✍

Love always as you set out on life together.

✍

Congratulations on your engagement and all the best for your
wedding day and your future together.

✍

Congratulations on your engagement. May God's blessings
be upon you both as you prepare for your life together.

✍

Congratulations and good wishes for your future.
Support and love always.

✍

May you have the best of life together - true happiness is a
treasure more precious than diamonds.

✍

There are preparations to be made.
Enjoy the lead-up to your special day.

✍

A ring on her finger—vows to be made -
not much longer until your special day.

We wish you all the happiness in the world together and
hope that all your dreams come true.

✍

Wishing you both a lifetime of joy and happiness.

✍

We hope your lives together will be happy
and your plans to wed go smoothly.

✍

The adorable couple, [name] and [name]

✍

Praying God's very best for you both.

✍

Wishing you a bright future filled with happiness.

✍

Congratulations on the exciting news.

✍

Hoping your future holds lots of wonderful surprises and experiences.

✍

Our wish is that your future brings the very best of everything.

✍

Wishing you love and luck for the plans that lie ahead.
May your future together be bright.

✍

With fondest love and heartfelt congratulations to both of you.

✍

May your joy together be timeless.

May your plans, dreams and preparations for a new life together
run smoothly. Have a wonderful engagement day.

✍

May your love, friendship and respect for each other
continue to grow as your big day approaches.

✍

Wishing you love and romance.

✍

May the months and years ahead be filled with much joy,
happiness and excitement.

✍

Congratulations, our highest hopes for this exciting and joy-filled year.

✍

We love you and would be so happy if we could help you in any way.

Kitchen Tea

I hope you will find a use for this gift in your new kitchen.
May you spend many happy hours there.

✍

All the best for success in the kitchen.

✍

I am sure this will come in handy. Have a lovely kitchen tea.

✍

I hope you have many happy days in your kitchen with friends and family.

✍

May your kitchen be a haven of love and comfort
for you and your new family.

✍

The kitchen is the heart of the home. May it be so in yours.

QUOTES

* *

'Warm kitchen, warm friends.'
—Czech saying

'When the stomach is full, the heart is glad.'
—Dutch proverb

Kitchen Tea

Marriage

'God, the best maker of all marriages,
Combine your hearts into one.'
—William Shakespeare (1564—1616),
Henry V

Congratulations. Best wishes for a lifetime of
love, happiness and special memories.

✍

The very warmest wishes and sincere congratulations.
May both of you enjoy your day of happy celebrations.

✍

Congratulations. Even though I'm on the other side
of the world, news still travels quickly.

✍

Congratulations on your marriage. We wish you much
happiness and that all your dreams come true.

✍

Congratulations on your marriage and we know God will
bless you through your many happy years together.

✍

Congratulations. It's wonderful to see you getting married as
you are perfectly suited—have a fantastic life together.

✍

Trust each other and you will be loyal; treat each other greatly
and you will each show yourselves great.

✍

It was once said that life can only be understood backwards, but it must be
lived forwards. May you go forward in leaps and bounds in your life together.

✍

May your life together be a time in which you prosper,
your friends are true and happiness is assured.

✍

May your love for each other and the dreams that you
share be a huge part of your lives.

Marriage

May your happiness and love for each other grow deeper
each day and make your lives together wonderful.

✍

May you share true contentment as husband and wife
each day of your life.

✍

May you always be lovers, but most of all friends.
Congratulations on your happy day.
May the joy of your love grow deeper with each anniversary.

✍

Our very best wishes for your wedding day
—long may the magic continue.

✍

May the Lord bless you richly in your new life together.
Look to him in every situation.

✍

Praying God's very best for you both.

✍

God bless you both richly on this special day.

✍

Love always, as you set out on a life together.

✍

This card comes with wishes for a happy day
and a happy life together.

✍

Wishing you both a lifetime of joy and happiness.

✍

May your life together be filled with happiness.

Wishing you all the joy and happiness that marriage brings.

✍

The adorable couple—enjoy the wonderful commitment you have made.

✍

We wish you all the happiness that life can bring your way.

✍

May your lives together hold everything you're dreaming of.

✍

You don't marry someone you can live with. You marry someone you can't live without. Congratulations.

MARRIAGE QUOTES

'Marriage is an authentic weaving together of families, of two souls with their individual fates and destinies, of time and eternity— everyday life married to the timeless mysteries of the soul.'
—Thomas More (1478—1535), English statesman and author

'Ever wonder why God gives us two? A right hand to show the left what to do. One ear to listen and one to hear the problems of others, their laughter and fears. One eye to watch and one to behold the beautiful treasures that life has to hold. One foot to travel and one to stand tall. Two feet to land on if we should fall. One man to stand by a woman's side; one woman to cherish being his bride. The love between partners comes shining through, and that is the reason God has made two. May God bless you on your wedding day.'
—Unknown

'In all of the wedding cake, hope is the sweetest of plums.'
—Douglas Jerrold (1803—57), English dramatist and writer

'Marriage is love personified.'
—Phoenix Flame, unknown

*'Marriage is the perfection of what love aimed at,
ignorant of what it sought.'*
  —Ralph Waldo Emerson (1803—82), US essayist and poet

*'Marriage—a book of which the first chapter is written
in poetry and the remaining chapters written in prose.'*
  —Beverly Nichols (1898—1983), British author

'One should believe in marriage as in the immortality of the soul.'
  —Honoré de Balzac (1799—1850), French novelist

*'When you make a sacrifice in marriage, you're sacrificing
not to each other but to unity in a relationship.'*
  —Joseph Campbell (1904—87), US writer

*'Marriage is not a simple love affair, it's an ordeal, and the ordeal is
the sacrifice of ego to a relationship in which two have become one.'*
  —Joseph Campbell (1904—87), US writer

'True it is that marriages be done in heaven and performed on Earth.'
  —William Painter (c. 1540—94), British author

'Marriage is our last, best chance to grow up.'
  —Joseph Barth, US clergyman

*'Married couples who love each other tell each other
a thousand things without talking.'*
  —Chinese proverb

*'There is no more lovely, friendly and charming relationship,
communion or company than a good marriage.'*
  —Martin Luther (1483—1586), German Protestant theologian

*'A good marriage is that in which each appoints the other guardian
of his solitude.'*
  —Rainer Maria Rilke (1875—1926), German poet and author

'What God hath joined together, let man not put asunder.'
  —Matthew 19:6

Anniversary

One rose for one lover; one friend, one inspiration,
producing many special moments.

✍

As the years have passed, our love has not diminished—
may our togetherness never fade with age.

✍

The day we met I knew our love was meant to be.
The day we married I knew it was for eternity.

✍

Thank you for the years we have spent together.
I feel so wrapped in your love.

✍

May the years we have left be blessed.

✍

If we could go back in time, not a thing would
I change—fate brought us together.

✍

You are the light of my days. I belong in your arms,
surrounded with love.

✍

Sitting here thinking of you, remembering all the time, love and
happiness we have shared. Thank you for all you have given me.
I love you more every day.

✍

Being without you is like a day without chocolate.
Happy anniversary!

Happy anniversary, darling! I'm the luckiest man in the world!

✍

Forever and always—that's how long I'll love you. Happy anniversary.

✍

You showed me love,
You made me feel whole,
You gave me happiness,
You make me complete.

✍

Happy anniversary, sweetheart! I'm the luckiest woman in the world!

✍

Anniversaries come and go, but our love continues forever.

✍

To my husband/wife—you are my sweetheart, my confidant
and adviser, my comforter and friend. You are my happy place
away from the rest of the world. Happy anniversary!

✍

To the one I love on our anniversary ... words will never be
able to express all I hold within my heart. You've made every
moment a happy memory. Happy anniversary!

TO ANOTHER COUPLE
ON THEIR ANNIVERSARY

Love brought you together as husband and wife ... and gave
each of you a best friend for life. Happy anniversary.

✍

May your heart be filled with love and your life with happiness.
Happy anniversary.

May you always be warmed by each other's smile,
Always take time to walk and talk a while,
Always know deep down you're each other's best friend,
And enjoy the kind of love that grows and knows no end.
Happy anniversary.

✍

May the warmth and love you bring to others
surround you both on your special day.

✍

'Music is love in search of a word.' You make such beautiful music
together. Happy anniversary!

✍

You have proved that love conquers everything.

✍

[Number] years and still going strong. Have a fabulous day.

✍

May today be filled with happy memories of the past and bright hopes
for the future. Happy anniversary to a wonderful couple.

✍

God gave you both a special love to share ... because he knew how
much you would cherish it. Happy anniversary.

✍

To a couple who really takes romance to heart. Have a wonderful day.

✍

To a beautiful pair on the birthday of your love affair.
Happy anniversary.

✍

We have seen the happiness that fills the home you've made.
Happy Anniversary

Your difference is what makes your love unique.
Congratulations on your anniversary.

✍

Faithful friends and partners. You're an inspiration to us all.

✍

Another year of a beautiful marriage. We have learned so much
from you as you have worked to make your love last.

✍

Your love has stood the test of time, no matter what has come your
way. You are both such an inspiration. Happy anniversary.

✍

It's such a joy to know two people so in love!
Happy anniversary to the special couple.

✍

There's no need to think about a second honeymoon—when there's no
evidence that you have even finished your first! Happy anniversary.

✍

Scientists have discovered that the longer people stay married,
the more they begin to look alike. You'd better start wearing name tags.
Happy anniversary.

ANNIVERSARY QUOTES

'Love seems the swiftest, but it is the slowest of all growths.
No man or woman really knows what perfect love is until
they have been married a quarter of a century.'
—Mark Twain (1835–1910), US author and humorist

'With 50 years between you and your well-kept wedding vow,
the Golden Age, old friends of mine, is not a fable now.'
—John Greenleaf Whittier (1807–92), US poet

New Baby

*'A baby was created
by the hand of God above,
To give the world the sweetest touch
of tenderness and love.'*

—Unknown

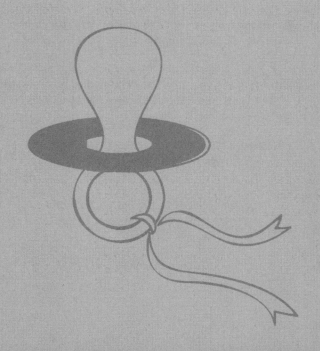

Our congratulations on the birth of your son/daughter.
We are very happy for you and wish you all the best.

✍

Congratulations on the arrival of your new daughter/son.
May God richly bless him/her always.

✍

Congratulations on your new arrival! Just remember—
babies are subject to change without notice!

✍

Welcome to the night shift! The hours are lousy, but
the benefits are great! Congratulations on your new baby.

✍

Congratulations on the arrival of [name].
We were so excited to hear your news.

✍

Congratulations on the birth of your new little baby.
Wishing you lots of fun times together as a family.

✍

Congratulations on your new baby. He/she has such beautiful
little fingers. You'll soon be wrapped around them.

✍

We were so pleased to hear everything went well
for you and your new little baby.

✍

Congratulations to you both and I hope
the little fella gives you years of joy.

✍

Congratulations on the first of many.

New Baby

Our love and thoughts are with you all on this wonderful event.

✍

May God richly bless you as you begin parenthood together.
We know that every day ahead of you will be the happiest kind.

✍

Congratulations on your 'Bundle of Joy'.

✍

At last he/she has arrived. Congratulations to you both.

✍

Glory be to God for the safe arrival of [name].
I am sure he/she will bring much joy to your hearts.

✍

You know what they say about babies—it's just one
damp thing after another! Congratulations.

✍

Dear Mummy and Daddy. Thank you for my baby sister/brother.
Love [name].

✍

This gift was purchased with much excitement on the birth of your baby
son/daughter [name]. With much love and congratulations.

✍

Your new baby is so blessed to have such fabulous
parents with so many wonderful qualities.

✍

The birth of your new son/daughter deserves the greatest celebration—
the very best wishes for your future together.

✍

Congratulations. May [name] bring you both all
the happiness in the world.

Dear [name]. Welcome. It's good to see you at last.

✍

Congratulations on the birth of [name]. May the Lord bless you with peace, happiness, health and safety.

✍

Congratulations on the birth of your little boy/girl. You must be very proud and overwhelmed. I wish you all a future full of love and happy memories.

✍

Congratulations on the birth of your beautiful son/daughter. I know he/she will bring you many cherished memories.

✍

A huge congratulations on your [weight] [name] . He/she is just adorable.

✍

We are very happy for you both. Congratulations to the proud parents and grandparents.

✍

Congratulations. Look after the baby and yourself too.

✍

Congratulations on your new bundle of love, small enough to hold in your arms, yet big enough to fill your whole life with joy.

✍

Congratulations. You guys did an excellent job. We look forward to spending time with your growing family in the years ahead.

✍

We pray all God's goodness for your little family. May he guide you as parents and keep you all safe and well. Thank goodness for disposables.

Congratulations, you must be filled with joy. Our love to you both and your new little boy/girl.

✍

The wonder of a new baby is the greatest gift of all.

✍

May your new son/daughter always be cradled in love and blessed with every happiness.

✍

A big welcome to baby [name]. May each new day bring new discoveries and surprises.

✍

Congratulations on your new baby, the first of many I'm sure. May this child open a whole new world of love, laughter and sleepless nights. May the Lord bless you greatly as a family and fill you both with his strength, joy and wisdom for all the exciting times ahead.

✍

We were delighted to hear of your successful productions. Well done.

✍

Congratulations. May you share the fun and work together.

✍

Congratulations on the arrival of your beautiful bundle of joy [name]. With all our love and best wishes.

✍

Congratulations on the new arrival to [address].

✍

The months of anticipation are finally over and the months of sleep deprivation ahead.

Wishing you all the best things for the new
little boy/girl who's just joined your family.

✍

You have a son/daughter [name]. That's fantastic.
Congratulations to you and love to your little boy/girl.

✍

Congratulations on your little baby boy/girl [name].
Take care of him/her. It's a jungle out there.

✍

[name] will fill your days with laughter and love and your home with
joy. With love to the happy family.

✍

Congratulations. We know you will find real love and
joy seeing your little son/daughter grow.

✍

I once heard the best way to give advice to your children is to find out
what they want and then advise them to do it. Happy parenting.

NEW BABY QUOTES

'Another miracle in this world. Welcome.'
  —Unknown

'Babies are such a nice way to start people.'
  —Unknown

'Every child is born a genius.'
  —R. Buckminster Fuller (1895—1983), US inventor and author

*'There are times when parenthood seems nothing
but feeding the mouth that bites you.'*
  —Peter De Vries (1910—93), US novelist
'Blessed are the young for they shall inherit the national debt.'
  —Herbert Hoover (1874—1964), former US president

'Children are the only form of immortality that we can be sure of.'
  —Peter Ustinov (1921—2004), British actor

'Parents are the bones upon which children sharpen their teeth.'
  —Peter Ustinov (1921—2004), British actor

'A baby is God's opinion that the world should go on.'
  —Carl Sandburg (1878—1967), US writer

Mother's Day

'When it comes to love, Mum's the word.'
—Unknown

Mum, you have been my inspiration. You have taught
me how to live and shown me how to love.

✍

All my good qualities I have learned from you.
Thank you for making me who I am.

✍

A mother's love is special. Thank you for always making me feel special.

✍

Where you are will always be home. Our feet may leave it,
but never our hearts. Happy Mother's Day.

✍

You've always been there for me—
my mother, my mentor and my friend.

✍

Before becoming a mother, I had a hundred theories on how to bring up
children. Now I have children and only one theory: love them, especially
when they least deserve to be loved. Thanks for all your love. Happy
Mother's Day.

✍

I love you, Mum—And this isn't the last time I'm going to tell you!
Happy Mother's Day.

✍

Mum, today's your day, so take it easy and relax.
You always seemed to know just what to do or what
to say to make my life so joyful and special.

✍

The precious moments you have given me
throughout my life will never be forgotten.

You gave me everything that has made me the person I am today.
Most of all, thank you for your unconditional love.

✍

Thank you for your loving kindness, your valuable wisdom
and your unconditional belief in me.

✍

In my heart, how could I ever forget my mother's love.
Your circle of love never ends.

✍

Thank you most of all for your love.

✍

There is no blessing quite so dear as a Mum like
you to love year after year! Happy Mother's Day.

✍

I just wanted to say how lucky I am to have a mother so beautiful inside
and out.

✍

Despite all of life's imperfections, you weave of it a world of joy and
wonder. With love on Mother's Day.

✍

To the best cookie-maker in the world.

✍

It's so hard for me to put together the words I want to say.
Just know that I love you this Mother's day.

✍

To my Mum, my friend, my confidant, happy Mother's Day.

✍

On Mother's Day, your children are supposed to cater to your every
whim—sort of goes against the natural order of things, doesn't it?

MOTHER'S DAY QUOTES

'All that I am or ever hope to be, I owe to my angel mother.'
—Abraham Lincoln (1809—65), former US president

'Of all the rights of women, the greatest is to be a mother.'
—Lin Yutang (1895—1976), Chinese author

'The most important thing a father can do for his children is to love their mother.'
—Unknown

'A man loves his sweetheart the most, his wife the best, but his mother the longest.'
—Irish proverb

'The heart of a mother is a deep abyss at the bottom of which you will always find forgiveness.'
— Honoré de Balzac (1799—1850), French novelist

'By and large, mothers and housewives are the only workers who do not have regular time off. They are the great vacationless class.'
—Anne Morrow Lindbergh (1906—2001), US writer and aviator

'The mother's heart is the child's schoolroom.'
—Henry Ward Beecher (1813—87),
    US Congregational clergyman

'Youth fades, love droops, the leaves of friendship fall; a mother's secret hope outlives them all.'
—Oliver Wendell Holmes (1809—94), US physician, poet and
    humorist

'A mother understands what a child does not say.'
—Jewish proverb

'Mother's love is peace. It need not be acquired, it need not be deserved.'
—Erich Fromm (1900—80), US psychoanalyst, born in Germany

'The hand that rocks the cradle is the hand that rules the world.'
    —William Ross Wallace (1819–81), US hymnwriter

'Her voice was ever soft, gentle and low, an excellent thing in woman.'
    —William Shakespeare (1564–1616), King Lear

'My mother was the most beautiful woman I ever saw.
All I am I owe to my mother. I attribute all my success in life
to the moral, intellectual and physical education I received from her.'
    —George Washington (1732–99), former US president

Mother's Day

Father's Day

'Blessed indeed is the man who hears many gentle voices call him father!'

—Lydia Maria Child (1802—80),
US abolitionist

Thank you for always being there when I need you. Happy Father's Day.

✍

Thank you for everything you do and all the warmth and love you share.

✍

I do not sing your praises as often as I should.
You are my protector, provider and hero.

✍

You are so wonderful in a million different ways.

✍

Daddy, I may be little but I love you real BIG! Happy Father's Day.

✍

Thank you for all the love and support you throw my way.

✍

You taught me:
Never give up
Reach for the stars
And take charge of your life.
You made my childhood special.

✍

Dad, you work so hard, you need a vacation from all
life's stress, demands, and overbearing egos. I'll try to get
out of the house for a while. Happy Father's Day.

✍

I know I can always count on you to be on my side.

✍

You have made so many sacrifices for me.
You are courageous, selfless and loving.

The good qualities you have given me will always be in style.

✍

Thank you for your amazing love and strength,
which made our house a home.

✍

Your strength and courage was such an important part of my life during
hard times.

✍

Thank you for forgiving me when I am wrong. Thank you for praising me
when I am right. But, most of all, thank you for being there for me.

✍

Dad, you've always given me everything I wanted. Either that or you're
very good at convincing me. Happy Father's Day.

✍

My Dad, my hero. Happy Father's Day.

✍

Happy Father's Day. I hope I've made you proud, Dad. And if not, hey,
maybe you ought to lower your expectations.

✍

Hope, love and peace to you this Father's Day.

✍

Happy Father's Day. You've always issued the law in our house, Dad, and
Mum carries it out. I guess that makes you an authority figurehead.

✍

Thank you for everything you have taught me.

✍

Not a day goes by that I don't feel loved by you.

Dear Dad, you always know what is on my mind. You're patient and helpful. Your love plays such a huge part in my life.

✍

Thank you for your love and support as I set out
to achieve my goals and dreams.

✍

You've always been a cut above the rest. Happy Father's Day.

✍

Each year that passes, I am more grateful that you are my Dad.

✍

You are the greatest man on Earth to me.
Thank you for keeping me grounded.

✍

Thank you for sharing all of life's lessons with me and teaching me
that hard work really does pay off. Happy Father's Day.

✍

Dad, as a tribute to you and your principles, I've always tried
to live my life by your time-honoured philosophy—
nothing's too good for my baby! Happy Father's Day.

✍

When I was little, Dad, I depended on you for my very existence. And
then I figured out how to turn the TV on myself. Happy Father's Day.

FATHER'S DAY QUOTES

'It is a wise father who knows his own child.'
  —William Shakespeare (1564—1616), *The Merchant of Venice*

'It doesn't matter who my father was;
it matters who I remembered he was.'
  —Anne Sexton (1928—1974), US poet

'One of the oldest human needs is having someone to wonder
where you are when you don't come home at night.'
  —Margaret Mead (1901—78), US anthropologist

'A man should have a child, plant a tree and write a book.'
  —Chinese proverb

Friendship

'I went outside to find a friend,
But could not find one there.
I went outside to be a friend,
And friends were everywhere.'

—Unknown

Thank you for being the sunshine that brightens my life.
You are a great friend.

✍

To my dearest friend. Thank you for being there for me. I feel
I can tell you everything and you would never criticise me.

✍

Thank you for all the wise advice you have given me. I wouldn't
be where I am today if it wasn't for your guidance.

✍

Through hard times and thick and thin,
I will always be there for you.

✍

To my newest friend. You can never have too many.

✍

Thank you for your support and listening ear. You are always
the first person I call. I am so grateful for our friendship.

✍

Just a quick note to express how much your friendship
means to me. Let's never take it for granted.

✍

Thank you for making me laugh when times are tough—
I couldn't get through it without you.

✍

To the most thoughtful person I know.
Thank you for your friendship.

✍

Whenever I am in need you are there—
thank you for your thoughtfulness.

A true friend is you.

Many people come in and out of my life, but only true friends leave footprints in my heart! Thank you for being a great friend.

Thank you for being a genuine friend ... one who is not afraid to say things, out of love, that are hard to say and hard to hear but cares enough to speak up.

You are a true friend.
We cry through the bad times,
we laugh through the good ...
with happiness and smiles,
with pain and tears,
I know you will be with me
throughout the years.

FRIENDSHIP QUOTES

*'A real friend is one who walks in
when the rest of the world walks out.'*
—Walter Winchell (1897–1972), US journalist and author

*'In prosperity our friends know us;
in adversity we know our friends.'*
—John Churton Collins (1848–1908), English literary critic

'A friend is one who sees through you and still enjoys the view.'
—Wilma Askinas (1926–), US author and columnist

Friendship

Thank You

Thanks [name] for everything you do, but mostly just for being you!

✍

Thank you for giving up your precious time to be involved in mine.
You are more than a friend—you are a friend that cares! Thanks again!

✍

You couldn't be nicer, I couldn't be happier,
and words couldn't thank you enough!

✍

With lives as busy as ours, we often forget the most
important people in them—so it's way past time I said
a very belated thank you for your kindness!

✍

Thanks for all the things you do and the really nice way you do them!

Thank You

Congratulations

Congratulations on your success. It is a
reflection of your strength and character.

✍

Congratulations. We are celebrating with you.

NEW HOME
● ●

Congratulations on your new home.
May it be filled with love and joy.

✍

May joy and peace be yours in your new home.

✍

Congratulations on your new home. May it be a
special place for friends, family and memories.

GRADUATION
● ●

Congratulations on making it to the end.

✍

We are so proud of you. We are looking forward
to seeing your prosperous future unfold.

✍

We are so proud of you and trust that wherever the road leads or whatever turn you decide to make it will be the right one.

✍

Best wishes for the future ... wherever it leads.
Congratulations on a huge milestone. Wishing you
lots of happiness on your graduation.

You have done your best. Be proud of all you have accomplished.

✍

Congratulations ... it's time to make your mark on the world.

✍

Wishing you joy and so much more on your graduation.

PROMOTION

Congratulations on your promotion.
I can't think of a more deserving person.

QUOTES

'When you've got it, flaunt it!'
—Zero Mostel, in the film *The Producers*

'Winning is not everything. It's the only thing.'
—Vince Lombardi (1913—1970), US pro football coach

'The happiest people in life don't have the best of everything ...
they make the best of everything they have.
Congratulations on doing the best of all!'
—Unknown

Christmas

Peace and joy at Christmas and throughout the New Year.

✍

Wishing you a Merry Christmas and a prosperous New Year.

✍

Merry Christmas and thank you for your friendship throughout the year.

✍

May love and joy be yours this Christmas time and into the New Year.

✍

Glory to God in the highest, and on Earth peace to all men.

✍

Joy to the world—and especially to you.

✍

This card brings love and wishes at Christmas time just for you.

✍

The season of peace, joy and sharing is here again.
To you and your family we send our love and best wishes.

✍

May your New Year be filled with health and prosperity.

✍

At this special time of year, warm wishes of love and peace
I send to you.

✍

Christmas is a special time to remember all those valuable times together.

✍

May your Christmas day be blessed with an
abundance of joy, peace and compassion.

When I think of you, it's Christmas every day.

✍

You are the decoration of my life. Merry Christmas!

✍

From our home to yours, we send love
and best wishes at this Christmas time.

✍

It only takes ONE good friend to brighten the whole season!
Merry Christmas!

✍

In the spirit of the season, may your holiday be filled with
joy, love and laughter. Merry Christmas.

✍

Abundant good wishes for happiness and joy this holiday season.

✍

May your treasures this Christmas be a home full of laughter, memories
and happiness, friendships rekindled and hearts filled with joy.

CHRISTMAS QUOTES

'At Christmas play and make good cheer,
For Christmas comes but once a year.'
    —Thomas Tusser (c. 1515—80), English author

'And is it true?
And is it true,
This most tremendous tale of all,
Seen in a stained-glass window's hue,
A Baby in an ox's stall?
The Maker of the stars and sea,
Became a Child on earth for me?'
    —Sir John Betjeman (1906—84), British poet

'I heard the bells on Christmas Day
Their old familiar carols play,
And wild and sweet the words repeat
Of peace on Earth, good will to men!'
    —Henry Wadsworth Longfellow (1807—82), US poet

'The feet of the humblest may walk in the field
Where the feet of the holiest trod,
This, then, is the marvel to mortals revealed.'
    —Phillips Brooks (1835—93), US Episcopal bishop

'Good news from heaven the angels bring,
Glad tidings to the earth they sing:
To us this day a child is given,
To crown us with the joy of heaven.'
    —Martin Luther (1483—1586), German Protestant theologian

'I heard the bells on Christmas Day
Their old, familiar carols play,
And wild and sweet the words repeat
Of peace on earth, good-will to men!'
    —Henry Wadsworth Longfellow (1807—82), US poet

'Somehow, not only for Christmas
But all the long year through,
The joy that you give to others
Is the joy that comes back to you.
And the more you spend in blessing
The poor and lonely and sad,
The more of your heart's possessing
Returns to you glad.'
   —John Greenleaf Whittier (1807–92), US poet

'I will honor Christmas in my heart, and try to keep it all the year.'
   —Charles Dickens (1812–70), English novelist

'Then ye be glad, good people,
This night of all the year,
And light ye up your candles:
His star is shining near.'
   —Unknown

'Love came down at Christmas,
Love all lovely, love divine;
Love was born at Christmas;
Star and angels gave the sign.'
   —Christina Georgina Rossetti (1830–94), British poet

'And she will bear a son, and you shall call his name Jesus,
for it is he who will save his people from their sins.'
   —Matthew 1:21

'Now when Jesus was born in Bethlehem of Judea in the days of
Herod the king, behold, there came wise men from the east to
Jerusalem, saying, where is he that is born King of the Jews? For we
have seen his star in the east, and are come to worship him.'
   —Matthew 2:1–2

'Happy, happy Christmas, that can win us back to the delusions of
our childhood days, recall to the old man the pleasures of his youth,
and transport the traveller back to his own fireside and quiet home!'
   —Charles Dickens (1812–70), English novelist

*'Blessed is the season which engages the whole world in
a conspiracy of love.'*
    —Hamilton Wright Mabie (1845–1916), US author

*'What is Christmas? It is tenderness for the past, courage for the
present, hope for the future. It is a fervent wish that every cup may
overflow with blessings rich and eternal, and that every path may
lead to peace.'*
    —Agnes M. Pharo, unknown

*'The joy of brightening other lives, bearing each others' burdens,
easing other's loads and supplanting empty hearts and lives with
generous gifts becomes for us the magic of Christmas.'*
    —W.C. Jones, unknown

*'Whatever else be lost among the years,
Let us keep Christmas still a shining thing:
Whatever doubts assail us, or what fears,
Let us hold close one day, remembering
Its poignant meaning for the hearts of men.
Let us get back our childlike faith again.'*
    —Grace Noll Crowell (1877–1969), US poet

Easter

Rejoice in the Lord! May all the beauty and glory of this blessed season
fill our hearts with praise. Happy Easter.

✍

Shout for joy, all the earth, lift up your voice and sing!
Christ the Lord is risen today. He reigns on high as King!
Wishing you a joyful, meaningful Easter.

✍

Alleluia! Christ is risen! Sharing with you the miracles
of new hope and new life. Have a joyous Easter.

✍

An Easter wish—May the glory of our living Lord renew your hopes,
your faith, your joy. Have a blessed Easter season.

✍

An Easter wish—On this day, may you experience
a sweet renewal of faith, hope, and joy.

✍

Easter greetings. Warmest wishes for a season of sweet discoveries.

✍

Easter is a time of remembrance. I will not forget you! Happy Easter.

✍

Thinking of you at Easter. Wishing you and those
you love the blessings of a glorious Easter.

✍

This special prayer at Easter-time is coming to convey,
the hope that all God's love and grace will light your Easter day!
Easter is a time of reflection and joy, when we emerge from our cocoon
of doubt to fly freely on the wings of faith. May you be renewed and
strengthened in the promise of our Lord.

For you—a wish for the happiest of Easters.

Remember, no matter how mature and sophisticated
you may become, you never outgrow
your need for chocolate bunnies! Happy Easter.

There's no time like Easter for remembering just how wonderful
God's love really is. Blessings to you and yours.

For you at Easter—May the joy of Christ's resurrection
live in your heart today and always.

Wishing you and those you love a joyous celebration of renewed faith.
Have a blessed Easter.

Easter celebrates God's gift of love: 'Neither height nor depth,
nor anything else in all creation, will be able to separate us
from the love of God.' (Romans 8:39) May you see his
mighty hand in every detail of your life. Happy Easter.

Get Well

*'He who has health has hope, but he
who has hope has everything.'*
—Arab proverb

Sorry you have not been well. Our thoughts and prayers
are with you for a speedy recovery.

✍

I feel bad that you feel bad—get well soon.

✍

Feelin' poorly? Well bless your heart—and every other little part!

✍

The doctor says you'll be back to normal soon—that'll be a first!
Get well soon!

✍

Looking forward to the return of your warm smile.

✍

We are praying you will be back to your wonderful self again
really soon.

GET WELL QUOTES

*'Your body is like a bar of soap. It gradually wears down from
repeated use.'*
—Dick 'Richie' Allen (1942—), US baseball player

'People who feel well are sick people neglecting themselves.'
—Jules Romains (1885—1972),
French novelist, playwright and poet

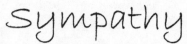

sympathy

'Death is not the last sleep.
It is the final awakening.'

—Walter Scott (1771–1832),
Scottish novelist

We know there is so little we can do to help you bear the pain of loss
you are feeling, and so little we can say to help you through the day.
But may you know our deepest love and sympathy are with you.

✍

Although we don't always understand, God has a purpose for all things
and he will not let things overwhelm us beyond what we can bear.
Our love and prayers for strength are with you.

✍

We are so sorry to hear of the loss of your beloved [name].
We pray that soon you will be able to heal your heart
with fond memories of the times you shared.

✍

It is so hard to bear the loss of someone you love.
All our love and sympathy goes out to you.

✍

We are thinking of you at this time of loss and
extend to you our sympathy and understanding.

✍

With thoughts of deep sympathy on the loss of your [name].
As time goes by, may the memories of the good times you shared
never fade.

✍

During this time of sorrow, know that we are thinking of you,
and may you find peace in the memories you hold.

✍

We are so sorry to hear of your loss. Words don't seem to say enough.
But we hope, in some small way,
they may help to ease the pain you are feeling.

Sympathy

There are no words to express the emptiness you must feel.
May fond memories be a comfort to you at this time
and may your heart soon be healed.

✍

At this sad time no words can convey what we feel for you.
We pray that your pain and emptiness may soon ease and
that these few words will be a comfort to you.

✍

At this sad and difficult time, our own hearts go out to you.
We are so very sorry to hear of your loss.

✍

Saying goodbye to someone so close is the hardest thing to endure.
May you find comfort in the words and love of those close to you.

✍

Losing a [name] is never easy. Please know we understand
your pain and are thinking of you during this difficult time.

✍

Our deepest sympathy at your time of loss.
We pray your sorrow grows lighter as the days go by.

✍

I know how difficult it is to say goodbye. I was so sorry to hear
of the loss of your beloved [name]. May memories of your
times together ease the ache in your heart.

✍

Our deepest sympathy to you and your family at this time.
May fond memories bridge the gap between you and [name].

✍

Words are not enough to express how sorry we were to hear of your
loss. May the precious memories you hold in your heart remain forever.

We were so sorry to hear of the loss of such a special person.
As the people who love you express their best wishes, may
you find comfort from the pain in your heart.

✍

May [name] live forever through the memories of those close to him/her.
Our love and deepest sympathy to you and your family.
It is so hard to say good bye to a loved one. May you find
comfort in the loving thoughts of those around you.

✍

Though we cannot fully share the pain you are feeling, you are always in
our thoughts and don't hesitate to call if there is anything you need.

SYMPATHY QUOTES

'The way through the world is more difficult to find than the way
beyond it.'
    —Wallace Stevens (1879—1955), US poet

'Earth hath no sorrow that heaven cannot heal.'
    —Thomas More (1478—1535), English statesman and author

'Better to light a candle than to curse the darkness.'
    —Chinese proverb

'To everything there is a season,
and a time to every purpose under heaven.'
    —Ecclesiastes 3:1

'The journey is the reward.'
    —Chinese proverb

'It is love, not reason, that is stronger than death.'
    —Thomas Mann (1875—1955), German novelist

'Love comforteth, like sunshine after rain.'
    —William Shakespeare (1564—1616), Venus and Adonis

Retirement

Now you can take time to smell the flowers,
catch up on some sleep and enjoy the sunshine.

✍

It's not retirement—just a longer weekend.

✍

You have done your time and proved yourself to be one of the best.
We are going to miss you.

✍

It's all smooth sailing for you now—enjoy it.

✍

Downhill—with no load. Enjoy the ride.

✍

It's time to stop watching the clock.

✍

It's a wonderful time in your life. Congratulations and all the best.

✍

You have earned the right to take time to enjoy yourself.

✍

Best wishes for your new phase of life.

✍

Look forward to the days ahead—have a wonderful time.

✍

It's the time in your life to stop and see what's new.

✍

May you pursue your future dreams with ambition and determination.

RETIREMENT QUOTES

'Working people have a lot of bad habits,
but the worst of these is work.'
—Clarence Darrow (1857—1938), US lawyer and debater

'Work is just another of man's diseases,
and prevention is better than cure.'
—Heathcote Williams (Born 1941), British playwright

'It is time I stepped aside for a less experienced and less able man.'
—US professor Scott Elledge (1914—1997),
on his retirement from Cornell University

Bon Voyage

'Until we meet again, may God hold you in the palm of his hand.'
—Irish blessing

May you prosper in everything you do and
wherever this journey takes you.

✍

We will miss your smiling face. Don't forget to
write or phone to let us know you are safe.

✍

Farewell on this new and exciting journey.

✍

Wherever you go, we know you will make an impression.

BON VOYAGE QUOTES

'I won't soon forget you.'
—Shane Garrett, unknown

'Love knows not its own depth until the hour of separation.
All farewells should be sudden.'
—Lord Byron (1788—1824), English poet

'Parting is such sweet sorrow
That I shall say good night till it be morrow.'
—William Shakespeare (1564—1616), Romeo and Juliet

'You look after your half of the world, and I will look after mine.'
—Shane Garrett, unknown

Apology

I am so sorry for what I have done. I will try to make it up
to you somehow. I hope our relationship is repairable.

✍

I will do anything to fix this mess I have made—
I am sorry for hurting you.

✍

I am so sorry for what I said and the way I have made you feel.
I didn't mean to hurt you.

✍

I hurt the one I love so much. I offer you my apology.
I am missing you so much—please forgive me.

✍

I am sorry for making you cry. I hurt because you hurt.
Can you ever forgive me?

Business

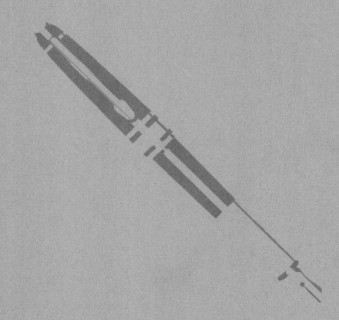

'What's worth doing is worth doing for money.'
   —Joseph Donahue, quoted in The Official Rule

'Money is the sixth sense that makes it possible
to enjoy the other five.'
   —Richard Ney (1915–2004),
      US actor, writer and investment adviser

'A billion here, a billion there, and soon
you're talking about real money.'
   —Everett Dirksen (1896–1969) US senator

'If you can count your money, you don't have a billion dollars.'
   —J Paul Getty (1892–1976) US oil industrialist

'If you don't drive your business you will be driven out of business.'
   —BC Forbes (1880–1954) US publisher

'I am opposed to millionaires, but it would be dangerous to offer me
the position.'
   —Mark Twain (1835–1910), American author and humorist

'A large income is the best recipe for happiness I ever heard of.'
   —Jane Austen (1775–1817), Northanger Abbey

Love Quotes

'To live without loving is to not really live.'
—Molière (1622—73), French comic playwright

'Love consists in this, that two solitudes protect and touch
and greet each other.'
—Rainer Maria Rilke (1875—1926), German poet and author

'We are shaped and fashioned by what we love.'
—Johann Wolfgang von Goethe (1749—1842), German author

'Take Spring when it comes and rejoice. Take happiness when it
comes and rejoice. Take love when it comes and rejoice.'
—Carl Ewald (1856—1908), Danish writer

'And think not you can guide the course of love.
For love, if it finds you worthy, shall guide your course.'
—Kahlil Gibran (1883—1931),
    Lebanese—US poet, philosopher and artist

'One man by himself is nothing. Two people who
belong together make a world.'
—Hans Margolius (1902—) German philosopher

'No love, no friendship, can cross the path of our destiny
without leaving some mark on it forever.'
—Francois Mauriac (1885—1970),
    French novelist and Nobel laureate

'Love does not consist in gazing at each other,
but in looking together in the same direction.'
—Antoine de Saint-Exupéry (1900—44), French pilot and poet

'The quarrels of lovers are like summer storms.
Everything is more beautiful when they have passed.'
—Suzanne Necker (1773—1794), French writer

'There is no remedy for love but to love more.'
—Henry David Thoreau (1817—1862)
    US author, poet and philosopher

'He who love touches walks not in darkness.'
  —Plato (427—347 BC), Greek philosopher

'The entire sum of existence is the magic of
being needed by just one person.'
  —Vii Putnam, US writer

'They gave each other a smile with a future in it.'
  —Ring Lardner (1885—1933), US writer

'Gather the rose of love whilst yet is time.'
  —Edmund Spenser (1552—1599), English writer and poet

'Treasure each other in the recognition that
we do not know how long we shall have each other.'
  —Joshua Liebman (1907—1948) US writer

'Perhaps love is the process of my gently leading you back to yourself.'
  —Antoine de Saint-Exupéry (1900—44), French pilot and poet

'Love is the only gold.'
  —Alfred Lord Tennyson (1809—1892) English poet

'Love is the greatest refreshment in life.'
  —Pablo Picasso (1881—1973), Spanish painter

'At the touch of love, everyone becomes a poet.'
  —Plato (427—347 BC), Greek philosopher

'Love is perhaps the only glimpse we are permitted of eternity.'
  —Helen Hayes (1900—1993), US actor

'To love and be loved is the greatest happiness of existence.'
  —Sydney Smith (1771—1845), English clergyman and essayist

'I beseech you now with all my heart definitely to let me
know your whole mind as to the love between us.'
  —William Shakespeare (1564—1616), *King Henry VIII*

'To love someone is to see a miracle invisible to others.'
— Francois Mauriac (1885—1970),
French novelist and Nobel laureate

'If you press me to say why I loved him, I can say
no more than it was because he was he and I was I.'
— Michel de Montaigne (1553—1592), French essayist

'The last of your kisses was ever the sweetest; the last smile
the brightest; the last movement the gracefullest.'
— John Keats (1795—1821), English poet

'I have spread my dreams beneath your feet;
Tread softly because you tread on my dreams.'
— W.B. Yeats (1865—1939) Irish poet, essayist and Nobel laureate

BIBLE LOVE QUOTES

'A new commandment I give unto you, that ye love one another;
as I have loved you, that ye also love one another.'
— John 13:34

'Love never faileth; but where there be prophecies, they shall fail;
where there be tongues, they shall cease, where there be
knowledge, it shall vanish away.'
— 1 Corinthians 13

'There is no fear in love; but perfect love casteth out fear.'
— 1 John 4:18

Funny Quotes

'Some mornings it just doesn't seem worth it
to gnaw through the leather straps.'
   —Emo Phillips, US comedian

'I try to take one day at a time, but sometimes
several days attack me at once.'
   —Ashleigh Brilliant (1933—), US humorist and cartoonist

'The Bible tells us to love our neighbours, and also to love our
enemies; probably because generally they are the same people.'
   — Gilbert Chesterton (1874—1936), English essayist,
      critic and author

'Only presidents, editors, and people with tapeworms
have the right to use the editorial "we"'.
   —Mark Twain (1835—1910), US author and humorist

'By all means marry. If you get a good wife, you'll be happy.
If you get a bad one, you'll become a philosopher
   —Socrates (469—399 BC), Athenian philosopher

'There are terrible temptations which it requires
strength and courage to yield to.'
   —Oscar Wilde (1854—1900), Irish dramatist and novelist

'Anyone who can only think of only one way
to spell a word obviously lacks imagination.'
   —Mark Twain (1835—1910), US author and humorist

'Everything is funny as long as it is happening to somebody else.'
   —Will Rogers (1879—1935), US actor and humorist

'All modern men are descended from worm-like creatures,
but it shows more on some people.'
   —Will Cuppy (1884—1949), US humorist and journalist

'The most important service rendered by the press is that of
educating people to approach printed matter with distrust.'
   —Samuel Butler (1612—1680) English poet and satirist

'The only way of catching a train I ever discovered
is to miss the train before.'
>   —Gilbert Chesterton (1874—1936) English essayist,
>   critic and author

'Bad spellers of the world—Untie!'
>   —Graffiti

'Always do right. That will gratify some of the people,
and astonish the rest.'
>   —Mark Twain (1835—1910), US author and humorist

'Three may keep a secret if two of them are dead.'
>   —Benjamin Franklin (1706—90), US statesman, diplomat,
>   author, scientist and inventor

'It is impossible to enjoy idling thoroughly
unless one has plenty of work to do.'
>   —Jerome K. Jerome (1859—1927) English humorist, novelist
>   and playwright

'Hanging is too good for a man who makes puns; he should be
drawn and quoted.'
>   —Fred Allen (1894—1956), US comedian

'Anyone who is considered funny will tell you, sometimes without
even your asking, that deep inside they are very serious, neurotic,
introspective people.'
>   —Wendy Wasserstein (1950—), US playwright

'It is better to keep your mouth shut and appear stupid
than to open it and remove all doubt.'
>   —Mark Twain (1835—1910), US author and humorist

'If I owned both Texas and Hell, I'd rent out Texas and live in Hell.'
>   —Philip Henry Sheridan (1831—1888), US general

'The reasonable man adapts himself to the world;
the unreasonable man persists in trying to adapt the world to himself.
Therefore, all progress depends on the unreasonable man.'
> —George Bernard Shaw (1856—1950), Irish dramatist, critic
> and novelist

'The power of accurate observation is commonly called cynicism by
those who have not got it.'
> —George Bernard Shaw (1856—1950), Irish dramatist, critic
> and novelist

'A man may be a fool and not know it, but not if he is married.'
> —H.L. Mencken (1880—1935), US journalist and critic

'What is the difference between a taxidermist and a tax collector?
The taxidermist takes only your skin.'
> —Mark Twain (1835—1910), US author and humorist

Cute Quotes

'If you can't be a good example, then you'll just have to be a horrible warning.'
    —Catherine Aird (1930—), English author

'Nothing is so useless as a general maxim.'
    —Lord Macaulay (1800—1859), English essayist, historian, poet and politician

'Education, like neurosis, begins at home.'
    —Milton R. Sapirstein (died 1996), US psychologist and author

'I could see that, if not actually disgruntled,
he was far from being gruntled.'
    —Pelham Grenville Wodehouse (1881—1975), English novelist

'The brain is a wonderful organ;
it starts working the moment you get up in the morning,
and does not stop until you get into the office.'
    —Robert Frost (1874—1963), US poet

'Do not take life too seriously; you will never get out of it alive.'
    —Elbert Hubbard (1856—1915), US author and publisher

'Never keep up with the Joneses. Drag them down to your level.
It's cheaper.'
    —Quentin Crisp (1908—1999), English writer

'Man has made use of his intelligence; he invented stupidity.'
    —Remy de Gourmont (1858—1915), French critic and novelist

'When people agree with me I always feel I must be wrong.'
    —Oscar Wilde (1854—1900), Irish dramatist and novelist

'The world is full of willing people; some willing to work,
the rest willing to let them.'
    —Robert Frost (1874—1963), US poet

'It's a dog-eat-dog world, and I'm wearing milk bone underwear.'
    —Norm, from the TV show *Cheers*

'It's not whether you win or lose, but how you place the blame.'
    —Anonymous

'It is inexcusable for scientists to torture animals; let them
make their experiments on journalists and politicians.'
    —Henrik Ibsen (1828—1906), Norwegian playwright and poet

'Many of us spend half our time wishing for things
we could have if we didn't spend half our time wishing.'
    —Alexander Woollcott (1887—1943), US author and journalist

Cute Quotes